Affirmations of the Soul
Volume One

Affirmations of the Soul
Volume One

Jack Armstrong
Author of *Lessons from the Source*

Wisdom from the Source Publications

Affirmations of the Soul, Volume One

Copyright © 2015 by Jack Armstrong

Jack Armstrong. (Affirmations of the Soul, Volume One)

Wisdom from the Source Publications

Printed in the United States of America

Belief consists in accepting the affirmations of the soul; unbelief, in denying them.

– Ralph Waldo Emerson

Friends,

In the section on affirmations *in Lessons from the Source,* you will find these words:

> *Affirmations are expressions of what you already know deep within you to be true. They affirm to the subconscious mind that it is doing the right thing by moving to bring good into your life. They also help reject the false concepts that have been planted in your mind by the mass consciousness. In effect, they are making the soil infertile for those negative seeds at the same time that they are providing fertile ground for the manifestation of your true desires.*

Affirmations have been part of the spiritual wisdom I've been receiving and transcribing since 1978, and this simple book is the first step in my commitment to sharing them with you. I trust that using them will help you remember the spiritual truths you already know and let go of any negativity that might be blocking your access to your good.

Much love and many blessings.

Jack Armstrong

——∞——

All is well, all is perfection,
and all my needs are met.

I am experiencing the blessings of the Kingdom as
I continue my earthly journey,
and my light is a beacon of goodness in the world.

I am richly blessed.

——∞——

———∞———

I am divinely guided, and the path is made clear.
Doors are open, and the path is made clear. I express
joy and enthusiasm in all that I do, and the path is
made clear.

I live each moment in joy and enthusiasm. My
essence is joy and enthusiasm. I am divinely guided in
every moment.

Doors are open, and the path is made clear.

———∞———

—∞—

I am open and receptive to miracles.

I expect them and eagerly anticipate
their manifestation in my life. All of my
needs are met – physical, emotional,
financial and health. I am free of any
concerns or doubts.

I am living in effortless perfection.

—∞—

—∞—

My life is goodness.

There is a never-ending fountain of blessings, and I drink from it and give thanks.

I am one with the Source of all creation, and I am its perfect expression.

Thank you, God.

—∞—

—∞—

I now pull myself out of despair. I let go of any and all negative attachments that are inhibiting my being fully in the flow. I am at one with the Source of all.

I am an expression of the Source of all goodness. I am free. I am liberated. There are no obstacles or restrictions or hindrances.

I am one with my good, and I am an expression of it.

—∞—

———∞———

I claim and accept and allow my perfect health, and I give thanks for it constantly. I am free, I am alive, I am in radiant and perfect health.

———∞———

—∞—

Nothing is difficult. Nothing is impossible.

The doors and windows of the Kingdom are open, and all its blessings and joys and miracles are mine.

All of the pieces are falling into place because I have let go, I am trusting God implicitly, and I allow perfection to unfold effortlessly in my life.

—∞—

—∞—

My creativity flows effortlessly in ways I never could have imagined. My very being is a beacon of God's goodness, and I effortlessly attract into my life those people to whom I can be a blessing, and also those who can be a blessing to me.

God's guidance is clear, his timing is perfect, and his supply is infinite. I shall never want – for financial supply, for creativity, for friendships, for perfect health, for perfect self expression. Miracles follow me and manifest in my life wherever I go.

I am blessed and a blessing.

—∞—

——∞——

I give thanks for this very moment, for it is all I can count on during my earthly journey. I see and feel and celebrate the wonder around me in the physical world.

This is the moment I have, and I live it.

——∞——

———∞———

As an eternal spiritual being, which is my true and simultaneous identity, all of my needs are always met, perfectly and effortlessly.

As I remind myself of this duality – human for awhile and spiritual forever – I can experience the blessings of the Kingdom while I still am experiencing my temporary journey in the physical world.

———∞———

———∞———

I am grateful for life, for the path I am on, for the experiences life has brought me, for the people and places I have known, for the gifts I have been given, for the guidance and love and nurturing and nudging that are always available.

I am free, and I am grateful.

———∞———

———∞———

I am alive with joy and enthusiasm. All my needs are being met. All things are working together for my highest good. I am blessed, and the endless flow of blessings carries me exactly where I need to go.

Fear is gone. Doubt is gone. Lack is gone. The need to prove myself is gone.

All negativity is now gone from my mind, emotions, body and life.

———∞———

———∞———

I do not allow the woes or travails of others to disturb me.

My conscious mind finally is remembering the truth of who I am, and it offers no resistance to my flow because of challenges others are facing in their own individual lives or how they are responding to them.

———∞———

———∞———

I am relaxed and at peace. There is no stress. I wake up each morning feeling joyous and enthusiastic and eager to see the blessings the day will bring.

I read and pray and meditate to center myself in my true beingness. I give thanks in advance for the blessings that already are here, but have not yet been made manifest.

———∞———

—∞—

I now claim and accept and call forth
into manifestation the following qualities
of God that are my true being. Because
limiting thoughts no longer have any
power over me, and never will again,
these qualities will rule my life for the rest
of my days in this incarnation: love, joy,
peace, enthusiasm, abundance, divine
order, divine guidance, hope, certainty,
perfection, flow, power, creativity.

—∞—

—∞—

I am one with the great creative force of the
Universe. I am its expression in physical or human
form. All that I say, think and do comes from Source.

I am an open, unobstructed channel for the expression
of God's goodness, wisdom and peace.

God's thoughts are my thoughts. God's words are my
words. God's goodness and perfection are
mine as well.

—∞—

——∞——

If this were my last day, none of the things
that have been bothering me would even be in
my consciousness.

This could be my last day, and I will live it – and
as many others as are left in my journey – in
celebration and joy and eager anticipation of the
infinite blessings of the Kingdom, for I am in it and
experiencing it now, in this moment, just as I have
and will throughout eternity.

I am blessed to be alive. Thank you, God!

——∞——

—∞—

I now center myself in the presence of God.

I am at peace, totally relaxed, and open to inspiration. I quiet my mind and allow it to rest. It has no need for conscious activity at this moment. It is as if I have flipped a switch, and it is off.

I am open and receptive to God's presence, God's guidance and direction, and God's blessings.

—∞—

—∞—

The fluctuations of my human emotions give way to the peace and presence of God, the Source of all creation.

My emotions are calmed by God's presence. I feel and allow and welcome God's expression of joy and enthusiasm and goodness in and through my entire being.

My joy is genuine, my serenity is pure, my love is never-ending.

I am a pure and perfect expression of God's essence, God's goodness, in the world and in my life.

—∞—

—∞—

I feel the light surrounding me, and I am grateful.
I feel, and I express, God's essence of joy and
peace and love and light and enthusiasm,
and I am grateful.

Nothing disturbs me. I am free, I am blessed, I am
in the flow of divine life.

All good things come my way.

—∞—

———∞———

I let go of the concept of time, for it relates either to the past or to the future.

In this instant, this moment of joy and peace and love, there is no time – there is only perfection, and I focus my attention and my energy on experiencing it and sharing it with the world.

———∞———

——∞——

I ask for guidance and direction, and I go with
the suggestions I am given.

I let go of my mind's bouts with uncertainty about
what I shall do or how I shall do it, and I ask for
and await and receive and give thanks for the
direction I receive.

——∞——

———∞———

I claim control of this day and of my life. My choices determine the state of my consciousness, and I choose life!

I choose joy, and my days are joyous. I choose love, and my being touches the very being of others. I choose peace, and my essence is calming. I choose light, and I am the light of the world.

———∞———

—∞—

I now let go of the struggle, for I do not need to make things happen.

I am free, and I cast the burden of stress and heaviness on God. I release it peacefully and effortlessly, knowing that there is a perfect outworking of every situation.

I have turned it over to God, and I am free.

—∞—

——∞——

I am open and receptive and obedient to the presence and power of God.

I am guided in every moment, and all my needs are met. I know, instinctively, what to do and when and how to do it.

The words I need and the thoughts I think flow smoothly and effortlessly to me, and I move ahead and take action without any conscious thought or struggle.

——∞——

—∞—

I am the light of the world.

I need do nothing more than let that light shine, for it is the essence of God. The woes and emotions of my human mind have no influence, no importance, no power over me, for I am experiencing the miracles of the Kingdom while still in human form.

I am free, and I release all concerns to God.

—∞—

—∞—

I now claim and accept the unlimited financial supply that is mine by divine right through my unity with God. God's supply is my supply.

I am entitled to that abundance as God's perfect expression, and I now release any and all resistance that my human mind has experienced and expressed of its own volition, and the channels are open, the windows of heaven are open, to my unlimited supply.

—∞—

—∞—

I am no longer burdened by the illusions my human mind has created.

I am free and unlimited – truly! – for I have released my human mind's need to be in control, and I allow, for the rest of my journey, my true spiritual beingness, which is my true identity, to take over and lead the way.

—∞—

— ∞ —

My joy is boundless.

My life is alive with goodness and blessings
and abundant supply. I am free of the past and
unconcerned about the future, and I live in the
glorious moment of now.

I am grateful for this moment in time.

— ∞ —

——∞——

I am well aware that any day, any moment, could be my last in physical form, and I move forward relishing each day and each moment and expressing the essence of God, absolutely certain that my desires are being made manifest in my life.

——∞——

—∞—

I am free, in all possible interpretations
of the word.

I am free of fear and worry and doubt and all other
negative emotions. I am free of the illusion of lack,
and I accept my abundant supply with ease
and with gratitude.

I am free to walk the path of my earthly journey in
light and in the expression of the essence of God. I
accept my freedom in its totality, and I live each
moment in gratitude.

Thank you, God!

—∞—

Other Books by Jack Armstrong:

Lessons from the Source:
A Spiritual Guidebook for Navigating Life's Journey

More Lessons from the Source:
Practical Wisdom for Enjoying Life's Journey

From the Source: An Introduction to Channeling

You Don't Need to Conduct the Orchestra:
Lessons on Letting Go, Trusting and Allowing

If you've found these affirmations to be helpful and would like to receive more, that's easy to do. *The Truth of You* is a free Monday morning e-mail with affirmations like these and previously unpublished excerpts from Jack Armstong's spiritual writings to help get your week off to a powerful and positive start.

To find out more and sign up, just visit:

www.lessonsfromthesource.com/truthofyou/

For more books by Jack Armstrong, please visit:

www.lessonsfromthesource.com/the-store/

www.ingramcontent.com/pod-product-compliance
Lightning Source LLC
Chambersburg PA
CBHW060544030426
42337CB00021B/4423